I0665510

STAND & DELIVER

TEN SHORT, HISTORIC SPEECHES TO PRACTICE AND LEARN

WITH NOTES & EXERCISES BY DAVE BRICKER

STAND & DELIVER
TEN SHORT, HISTORIC SPEECHES TO PRACTICE AND LEARN

All rights reserved. No part of this book may be reproduced or transmitted in any form or by any means, electronic or mechanical, including photocopying, recording, or by an information storage and retrieval system — except by a reviewer who may quote brief passages in a review to be printed in a magazine or newspaper — without permission in writing from the publisher.

Though the island settings in this book are based on actual places, the narrative is a work of fiction. Characters, names, businesses, places, and events are wholly fictitious. Any resemblance to actual persons, living or dead, or to actual events is purely coincidental.

ESSENTIAL ABSURDITIES PRESS

Copyright 2019 Essential Absurdities Press
Book design and production by Dave Bricker

ISBN: 978-0-9862960-5-5

*"Vary the pose and vary the pitch.
Finally, don't forget the pause."*
— Winston Churchill

Contents

Introduction I

How to Use this Book 5

Abraham Lincoln: Gettysburg Address 11

    Worksheet: Abraham Lincoln 15

Winston Churchill: We Shall Fight on the Beaches 21

    Worksheet: Winston Churchill 25

Josephine Baker: March on Washington 33

    Worksheet: Josephine Baker 37

John F. Kennedy: Inaugural Address 43

    Worksheet: John F. Kennedy 47

William Lyon Phelps: A Borrowed Book 57

    Worksheet: William Lyon Phelps 61

Lou Gehrig: Farewell to Baseball ' 69

    Worksheet: Lou Gehrig 73

General Douglas MacArthur: Duty, Honor, Country............ 79

    Worksheet: Douglas MacArthur... 83

Patrick Henry: Give Me Liberty or Give Me Death 91

    Worksheet: Patrick Henry.. 97

Susan B Anthony: Are Women Persons? 103

    Worksheet: Susan B. Anthony... 105

Sojourner Truth: Ain't I a Woman? 109

    Worksheet: Sojourner Truth 113

Final Exercise... 121

About the Author 123

Other Books by Dave Bricker 125

Introduction

*A*s a speaker hoping to advance my skills, I attended an acting workshop. I watched, mesmerized, as actors presented monologues and the instructor, Tom Todoroff, coached them. Their performances improved remarkably.

But I am not an actor—at least not in the traditional, dramatic, theatrical sense. As I watched these proceedings, I wondered, *How can I apply these principles to the world of public speaking? If I were to attend this workshop again, what could I present that would help me advance as a speaker?*

During the workshop, Tom proposed that the serious actor should have several monologues "in their back pocket," ready to present at an audition or workshop. Adapting this advice, I searched for short speeches that presenters could study, practice, and deliver—on their own or with a coach.

None of the selection of short (the longest is 419 words), historic speeches and excerpts in this book were derived from dramatic productions. While actors generally speak to one another "behind the fourth wall,"[1] these orators spoke directly to their audiences. Hence these "monologues" were especially selected to benefit speakers.

Some, like Abraham Lincoln's iconic "Gettysburg Address," are profoundly eloquent, while Josephine Baker's "March on Washington" speech and Lou Gehrig's "Farewell to Baseball" are humbly stated and heartfelt.

Three of the ten speeches in this book were authored by women. Male speakers, use these works to expand your range. Female speakers (who must rely on a male-dominated canon of historic speeches) will find additional motivation here to advance their skills.

Each presentation is short enough to memorize with minimal effort. In keeping with this objective, many of the selections are excerpts from longer speeches. Add vocal variety and body language, either to imitate and learn from the original speaker or to recraft the speech in your own style. Either approach will grow your platform skills.

1. Fourth wall — the imaginary wall between the audience and the world portrayed on the stage.

Capture the eloquence of William Phelps and the "down-home southern grit" of Sojourner Truth. Imagine yourself as Abraham Lincoln standing on a platform at the edge of a muddy battlefield, sharing his message in the days before microphones and speakers. How must John F. Kennedy have felt on that cold inauguration day in 1961 when he took the helm of a nation threatened by a nuclear arms race?

Whether you speak on the platform or in the conference room, the classroom, or the bathroom, the speeches and exercises in this book will challenge you to look deep into words and meanings, and prepare you emotionally and technically to "stand and deliver."

How to Use this Book

*E*ach of the speech selections is presented twice.

The first instance includes historical context and a transcript of the speech or excerpt as it was written.

The second version breaks the selection down into short lines and phrases. Use the spaces in-between to insert stage directions and notes.

Transcripts of these speeches can be found online. If it suits you, download a copy and work in your word processor.

Work on your own or with an acting or storytelling coach who understands the fine art of interpreting a script.

In a few instances, to prevent "stumbling" over unfamiliar words, spelling has been updated to reflect contemporary English. "Today" was once hyphenated: "to-day." "Cannot" was originally two words: "can not." "Congress" was once spelled, "Congrefs." Such obstacles to easy reading have been eliminated.

Emphasis

Experiment with adding and changing emphasis by underlining or highlighting certain words. Use a pencil so your choices can be easily modified.

I pledge allegiance to the <u>flag</u> of the United States of America...

conveys a different meaning than

I pledge allegiance to the flag of the <u>United States of America</u>...

Use single, double, or triple underlines to suggest varying degrees of emphasis.

Some speakers sound out every word or phrase to test the impact of emphasizing each:

<u>I</u> pledge allegiance to the flag of the United States of America...
I <u>pledge</u> allegiance to the flag of the United States of America...
I pledge <u>allegiance</u> to the flag of the United States of America...
I pledge allegiance <u>to</u> the flag of the United States of America...
I pledge allegiance to the <u>flag</u> of the United States of America...
I pledge allegiance to the flag <u>of</u> the United States of America...
I pledge allegiance to the flag of the <u>United States of America</u>...

Pauses

Insert vertical lines to indicate short and long pauses, like so:

> The hardest thing to live with is regret.
> The hardest thing to live with | is regret.
> The hardest thing to live with ‖ is regret.

Or add an approximate number of seconds under a single pause line, like so:

> The hardest thing to live with | is regret.
>   2

Stage Directions

Insert stage directions, gestures, and notes about vocal inflections above and below the lines of the speech, like so:

> *Move to the right side of the stage (audience's left) to start the journey*
> I began my journey over twenty years ago…

Consider Lincoln's Gettysburg address as an example:

> *Expand hands*
> But, in a larger sense

Add growing vocal emphasis to each of the three words

we cannot <u>dedicate</u>—

Right fist into left palm

we cannot <u>consecrate</u>—

Right fist into left palm (harder)

we cannot <u>hallow</u>—this ground.

Right fist into left palm (even harder), open arms downward to gesture toward the field

Imitation or Innovation?

Well-written words were not always eloquently delivered. "We shall fight on the beaches…" was part of a much longer address to Parliament. As capable an orator as Winston Churchill may have been, it will never be known whether he was tired at the end of a long presentation, deprived of sleep by war duties, or just having an off-day. His words were brilliant, but his delivery was lackluster. Will you imitate Churchill's "cottonballs-in mouth" style and his British accent, or will you reimagine his speech in a way that reflects your own style?

Will you deliver Sojourner Truth's speech in the vernacular (It's difficult not to given that the script contains words like "ain't") or will you "polish" it?

Will Lou Gehrig's Farewell Address convey the same sincerity if delivered as a lofty, erudite presentation? Can you deliver this speech authentically in "plain folks" style?

How will you interpret Abraham Lincoln's Gettysburg Address, given that no audio recordings of it exist?

There is no one best, right way. Imitate or Innovate. Links to source transcripts, recordings, and videos are provided as footnotes and copies of the selections are available at https://storysailing.com/short-speeches-book. Avail yourself of these resources or work straight from the book. Interpret these speeches in any way that inspires you to think deeply about words and gestures, stretches your range, and grows your oratory skill.

Abraham Lincoln:
Gettysburg Address[2,3]

November 19, 1863 (268 words)

Abraham Lincoln came to Gettysburg, the scene of a ferocious Civil War battle, to unite America when it had been divided by different views of the war, to restate his view of the purpose of the United States, and to provide direction for the country. Lincoln's short speech followed Edward Everett's *long* presentation. After the ceremony, Everett remarked, "I should be glad if I could flatter myself that I came as near to the central idea of the occasion in two hours as you did in two minutes." Note that this speech predates the use of electronic amplification and recording technology.

2. http://passionforthepast.blogspot.com/2013/11/president-lincoln-at-gettysburg-first.html

3. https://youtu.be/fU6UacteZus

Eyewitness Account

"As Lincoln spoke, he had one hand on each side of his manuscript (and) spoke in a most deliberate manner, and with such a forceful and articulate expression that he could be heard by all of that immense throng," Philip Bikle recalled. "There was no gesture except with both hands up and down, grasping the manuscript which he did not seem to need, as he looked at it so seldom." Several newspapers noted that the speech was interrupted by applause five times.

The Speech

Four score and seven years ago our fathers brought forth on this continent, a new nation, conceived in Liberty, and dedicated to the proposition that all men are created equal.

Now we are engaged in a great civil war, testing whether that nation, or any nation so conceived and so dedicated, can long endure. We are met on a great battlefield of that war. We have come to dedicate a portion of that field, as a final resting place for those who here gave their lives that that nation might live. It is altogether fitting and proper that we should do this.

But, in a larger sense, we cannot dedicate—we cannot consecrate—we cannot hallow—this ground. The brave men, living and dead, who struggled here, have consecrated it far above our poor power to add or detract. The world will little note, nor long remember what we say here, but it can never forget what they did here. It is for us the living, rather, to be dedicated here to the unfinished work which they who fought here have thus far so nobly advanced. It is rather for us to be here dedicated to the great task remaining before us—that from these honored dead we take increased devotion to that cause for which they gave the last full measure of devotion—that we here highly resolve that these dead shall not have died in vain—that this nation, under God, shall have a new birth of freedom—and that government of the people, by the people, for the people, shall not perish from the earth.

Worksheet: Abraham Lincoln

_____

_____

Four score and seven years ago

_____

_____

our fathers brought forth on this continent,

_____

_____

a new nation,

_____

_____

conceived in Liberty,

_____

_____

and dedicated to the proposition

_____

_____

that all men are created equal.

_____

_____

Now we are engaged in a great civil war,

_____

_____

testing whether that nation,

_____

_____

or any nation so conceived and so dedicated,

_____

_____

can long endure.

_____

_____

We are met on a great battle-field of that war.

_____

_____

We have come to dedicate a portion of that field,

_____

_____

as a final resting place

_____

_____

for those who here gave their lives

_____

_____

that that nation might live.

_____

_____

It is altogether fitting and proper that we should do this.

_____

_____

But, in a larger sense,

_____

_____

we cannot dedicate—

_____

_____

we cannot consecrate—

_____

_____

we cannot hallow—this ground.

_____

_____

The brave men,

_____

_____

living and dead,

_____

_____

who struggled here,

have consecrated it

far above our poor power to add or detract.

The world will little note,

nor long remember what we say here,

but it can never forget what they did here.

It is for us the living, rather,

to be dedicated here to the unfinished work

which they who fought here have thus far so nobly advanced.

_____

_____

It is rather for us to be here dedicated

_____

_____

to the great task remaining before us—

_____

_____

that from these honored dead

_____

_____

we take increased devotion

_____

_____

to that cause for which they gave

_____

_____

the last full measure of devotion—

_____

_____

that we here highly resolve that these dead

_____

_____

shall not have died in vain—

that this nation,

under God,

shall have a new birth of freedom —

and that government of the people,

by the people,

for the people,

shall not perish from the earth.

Winston Churchill:

We Shall Fight on the Beaches[4,5]

(308 words)

"We Shall Fight on the Beaches" is a small portion of a longer speech delivered by Winston Churchill to the House of Commons of the Parliament of the United Kingdom on June 4, 1940 during the second Word War. Though his words were brilliant and inspiring, Churchill's delivery was less so despite his usual facility.

Work on "We Shall Fight on the Beaches" with or without a British accent. How would you have delivered the speech? How might Churchill have delivered it on a better day?

4. https://winstonchurchill.org/resources/speeches/1940-the-finest-hour/we-shall-fight-on-the-beaches/

5. https://www.youtube.com/watch?v=MkTw3_PmKtc

The Speech (excerpted)

I have, myself, full confidence that if all do their duty, if nothing is neglected, and if the best arrangements are made, as they are being made, we shall prove ourselves once again able to defend our island home, to ride out the storm of war, and to outlive the menace of tyranny, if necessary for years, if necessary alone. At any rate, that is what we are going to try to do. That is the resolve of His Majesty's Government—every man of them. That is the will of Parliament and the nation. The British Empire and the French Republic, linked together in their cause and in their need, will defend to the death their native soil, aiding each other like good comrades to the utmost of their strength. Even though large tracts of Europe and many old and famous states have fallen or may fall into the grip of the Gestapo and all the odious apparatus of Nazi rule, we shall not flag or fail. We shall go on to the end, we shall fight in France, we shall fight on the seas and oceans, we shall fight with growing confidence and growing strength in the air, we shall defend our island, whatever the cost may be, we shall fight on the beaches, we shall fight on the landing grounds, we shall fight in the fields and in the streets, we shall fight in the hills; we shall never surrender, and even if, which I do not for a moment believe, this island or a large part of it were subjugated and starving, then our empire beyond the seas, armed and guarded by the British fleet, would carry on the struggle, until, in God's good time, the New World, with all its power and might, steps forth to the rescue and the liberation of the old.

Worksheet: Winston Churchill

_____

_____

I have, myself, full confidence

_____

_____

that if all do their duty,

_____

_____

if nothing is neglected,

_____

_____

and if the best arrangements are made,

_____

_____

as they are being made,

_____

_____

we shall prove ourselves once again able

_____

_____

to defend our island home,

to ride out the storm of war,

and to outlive the menace of tyranny,

if necessary for years,

 if necessary alone.

At any rate, that is what we are going to try to do.

That is the resolve of His Majesty's Government—

every man of them.

That is the will of Parliament and the nation.

_____

_____

The British Empire and the French Republic,

_____

_____

linked together in their cause and in their need,

_____

_____

will defend to the death their native soil,

_____

_____

aiding each other like good comrades

_____

_____

to the utmost of their strength.

_____

_____

Even though large tracts of Europe

_____

_____

and many old and famous states have fallen or may fall

_____

_____

into the grip of the Gestapo

and all the odious apparatus of Nazi rule,

we shall not flag or fail.

We shall go on to the end,

we shall fight in France,

we shall fight on the seas and oceans,

we shall fight with growing confidence

and growing strength in the air,

we shall defend our island,

———————————————————————————

———————————————————————————

whatever the cost may be,

———————————————————————————

we shall fight on the beaches,

———————————————————————————

we shall fight on the landing grounds,

———————————————————————————

we shall fight in the fields

———————————————————————————

and in the streets,

———————————————————————————

we shall fight in the hills;

———————————————————————————

we shall never surrender,

———————————————————————————

and even if,

---

which I do not for a moment believe,

---

this island or a large part of it

---

were subjugated and starving,

---

then our empire beyond the seas,

---

armed and guarded by the British fleet,

---

would carry on the struggle,

---

until, in God's good time,

---

the New World,

_____

_____

with all its power and might,

_____

_____

steps forth to the rescue

_____

_____

and the liberation of the old.

Josephine Baker:
March on Washington[6]
(316 words)

Josephine Baker was a showgirl in 1920s and '30s Paris who retired her skimpy costumes to serve in the French Resistance before becoming an international superstar. She was the only woman to speak at Dr. Martin Luther King, Jr.'s "March on Washington" in 1963. The 57-year-old Baker flew in from France for the event. Having left school in sixth grade, she was not entirely comfortable speaking publicly. Her speech relied on simple language and natural charisma.

---

6. http://openvault.wgbh.org/catalog/A_F04F9F2C56AE49738BFA0DA1089A09C5 (search for "Baker" and then play the audio.)

The Speech (excerpted)

And when I got to New York way back then, I had other blows—when they would not let me check into the good hotels because I was colored, or eat in certain restaurants. And then I went to Atlanta, and it was a horror to me. And I said to myself, My God, I am Josephine, and if they do this to me, what do they do to the other people in America?

You know, friends, that I do not lie to you when I tell you I have walked into the palaces of kings and queens and into the houses of presidents—and much more. But I could not walk into a hotel in America and get a cup of coffee, and that made me mad. And when I get mad, you know that I open my big mouth. And then look out, 'cause when Josephine opens her mouth, they hear it all over the world.

So I did open my mouth, and you know I did scream, and when I demanded what I was supposed to have and what I was entitled to, they still would not give it to me.

So then they thought they could smear me, and the best way to do that was to call me a communist. And you know, too, what that meant. Those were dreaded words in those days, and I want to tell you also that I was hounded by the government agencies in America, and there was never one ounce of proof that I was a communist. But they were mad. They were mad because I told the truth. And the truth was that all I wanted was a cup of coffee. But I wanted that cup of coffee where I wanted to drink it, and I had the money to pay for it, so why shouldn't I have it where I wanted it?

Worksheet: Josephine Baker

_____

_____

And when I got to New York way back then,

_____

_____

I had other blows—

_____

_____

when they would not let me check into the good hotels

_____

_____

because I was colored,

_____

_____

or eat in certain restaurants.

_____

_____

And then I went to Atlanta,

_____

_____

and it was a horror to me.

_____

_____

And I said to myself,

_____

_____

My God, I am Josephine,

_____

_____

and if they do this to me,

_____

_____

what do they do to the other people in America?

_____

_____

You know, friends, that I do not lie to you

_____

_____

when I tell you I have walked into the palaces of kings and queens

_____

_____

and into the houses of presidents —

_____

_____

and much more.

But I could not walk into a hotel in America

and get a cup of coffee,

and that made me mad.

And when I get mad, you know that I open my big mouth.

And then look out,

'cause when Josephine opens her mouth,

they hear it all over the world.

So I did open my mouth,

and you know I did scream,

and when I demanded what I was supposed to have

and what I was entitled to,

they still would not give it to me.

So then they thought they could smear me,

and the best way to do that was to call me a communist.

And you know, too, what that meant.

Those were dreaded words in those days,

_____

_____

and I want to tell you also

_____

_____

that I was hounded by the government agencies in America,

_____

_____

and there was never one ounce of proof that I was a communist.

_____

_____

But they were mad.

_____

_____

They were mad because I told the truth.

_____

_____

And the truth was that all I wanted was a cup of coffee.

_____

_____

But I wanted that cup of coffee where I wanted to drink it,

_____

_____

and I had the money to pay for it,

_____

_____

so why shouldn't I have it where I wanted it?

John F. Kennedy:
Inaugural Address [7]

(378 words)

*I*n his 1961 inaugural address, John F. Kennedy challenged America to join him in the struggle for freedom during the Cold War. Nearly a million people braved freezing temperatures to see the new President. The issues of the day—the Communist threat, a nuclear arms race, racial unrest, and economic distress—awaited him and the nation. JFK's inaugural address had to instill confidence at home and respect abroad.

Kennedy was a war veteran—a combat hero. He had read the great speeches of the ages, and believed in the power of words. He believed that democracy thrives only when citizens contribute their talents to the common good, and that it is up to leaders to inspire acts of sacrifice.

7. https://www.youtube.com/watch?v=PEC1C4p0k3E

The Speech (excerpted)

The world is very different now. For man holds in his mortal hands the power to abolish all forms of human poverty and all forms of human life. And yet the same revolutionary beliefs for which our forebears fought are still at issue around the globe — the belief that the rights of man come not from the generosity of the state but from the hand of God.

We dare not forget today that we are the heirs of that first revolution. Let the word go forth from this time and place, to friend and foe alike, that the torch has been passed to a new generation of Americans — born in this century, tempered by war, disciplined by a hard and bitter peace, proud of our ancient heritage — and unwilling to witness or permit the slow undoing of those human rights to which this nation has always been committed, and to which we are committed today at home and around the world.

Let every nation know, whether it wishes us well or ill, that we shall pay any price, bear any burden, meet any hardship, support any friend, oppose any foe to assure the survival and the success of liberty.

This much we pledge — and more.

   ...

Now the trumpet summons us again — not as a call to bear arms, though arms we need — not as a call to battle, though embattled we are—but a call to bear the burden of a long twilight struggle, year in and year out, "rejoicing in hope, patient in tribulation"—a struggle against the common enemies of man: tyranny, poverty, disease and war itself....

In the long history of the world, only a few generations have been granted the role of defending freedom in its hour of maximum danger. I do not shrink from this responsibility—I welcome it. I do not believe that any of us would exchange places with any other people or any other generation. The energy, the faith, the devotion which we bring to this endeavor will light our country and all who serve it—and the glow from that fire can truly light the world.

And so, my fellow Americans: ask not what your country can do for you—ask what you can do for your country.

Worksheet: John F. Kennedy

_____

_____

The world is very different now.

_____

_____

For man holds in his mortal hands

_____

_____

the power to abolish all forms of human poverty

_____

_____

and all forms of human life.

_____

_____

And yet the same revolutionary beliefs for which our forebears
fought

_____

_____

are still at issue around the globe —

_____

_____

the belief that the rights of man

come not from the generosity of the state

but from the hand of God.

We dare not forget today

that we are the heirs of that first revolution.

Let the word go forth from this time and place,

to friend and foe alike,

that the torch has been passed

to a new generation of Americans—

born in this century,

tempered by war,

disciplined by a hard and bitter peace,

proud of our ancient heritage —

and unwilling to witness or permit

the slow undoing of those human rights

to which this nation has always been committed,

and to which we are committed today at home

_____

_____

and around the world.

_____

_____

   Let every nation know,

_____

_____

whether it wishes us well or ill,

_____

_____

that we shall pay any price,

_____

_____

bear any burden,

_____

_____

meet any hardship,

_____

_____

support any friend,

_____

_____

oppose any foe

to assure the survival and the success of liberty.

This much we pledge — and more.

   Now the trumpet summons us again —

not as a call to bear arms,

though arms we need —

not as a call to battle,

though embattled we are —

but a call to bear the burden

of a long twilight struggle,

year in and year out,

"rejoicing in hope,

patient in tribulation"—

a struggle against the common enemies of man:

tyranny,

poverty,

disease

and war itself....

In the long history of the world,

only a few generations

have been granted the role

of defending freedom in its hour of maximum danger.

I do not shrink from this responsibility—

I welcome it.

I do not believe that any of us would exchange places

with any other people or any other generation.

The energy,

the faith,

the devotion which we bring to this endeavor

will light our country and all who serve it—

and the glow from that fire

can truly light the world.

And so, my fellow Americans:

_____

_____

ask not what your country can do for you—

_____

_____

ask what you can do for your country.

William Lyon Phelps:
A Borrowed Book[8]

(419 words)

William Lyon Phelps (1865-1943) was an American educator, literary critic and author. On April 6, 1933, in response to the Nazi burning of books containing "un-German" ideas, he delivered the following radio address:

The Speech (excerpted)

The habit of reading is one of the greatest resources of mankind; and we enjoy reading books that belong to us much more than if they are borrowed. A borrowed book is like a guest in the house; it must be treated with punctiliousness, with a certain considerate formality. You must see that it sustains no damage; it must not

8. http://www.historyplace.com/speeches/phelps.htm

suffer while under your roof. You cannot leave it carelessly, you cannot mark it, you cannot turn down the pages, you cannot use it familiarly. And then, some day, although this is seldom done, you really ought to return it.

But your own books belong to you; you treat them with that affectionate intimacy that annihilates formality. Books are for use, not for show; you should own no book that you are afraid to mark up, or [are] afraid to place on the table, wide open and face down. A good reason for marking favorite passages in books is that this practice enables you to remember more easily the significant sayings, to refer to them quickly, and then in later years, it is like visiting a forest where you once blazed a trail. You have the pleasure of going over the old ground, and recalling both the intellectual scenery and your own earlier self.

...

There are of course no friends like living, breathing, corporeal men and women; my devotion to reading has never made me a recluse. How could it? Books are of the people, by the people, for the people. Literature is the immortal part of history; it is the best and most enduring part of personality. But book-friends have this advantage over living friends; you can enjoy the most truly aristocratic society in the world whenever you want it. The great dead are beyond our physical reach, and the great living are usually almost as inaccessible; as for our personal friends and acquaintances, we cannot always see them. Perchance they are asleep, or away on a journey. But in a private library, you can at any moment converse with Socrates or Shakespeare or Carlyle or Dumas or Dickens or Shaw or Barrie or Galsworthy. And there is no doubt that in these books you see these men at their best. They wrote for *you*. They "laid themselves out," they did their ultimate best to entertain you, to make a favorable impression. You are necessary to them as an audience is to an actor; only instead of seeing them masked, you look into their innermost heart of heart[s].

Worksheet: William Lyon Phelps

The habit of reading is one of the greatest resources of mankind;

---

and we enjoy reading books that belong to us

---

much more than if they are borrowed.

A borrowed book is like a guest in the house;

---

it must be treated with punctiliousness,

---

with a certain considerate formality.

You must see that it sustains no damage;

_____

_____

it must not suffer while under your roof.

_____

_____

You cannot leave it carelessly,

_____

_____

you cannot mark it,

_____

_____

you cannot turn down the pages,

_____

_____

you cannot use it familiarly.

_____

_____

And then, some day,

_____

_____

although this is seldom done,

_____

_____

you really ought to return it.

But your own books belong to you;

you treat them with that affectionate intimacy

that annihilates formality.

Books are for use, not for show; y

ou should own no book that you are afraid to mark up,

or [are] afraid to place on the table,

wide open and face down.

A good reason for marking favorite passages in books

is that this practice enables you to remember more easily

the significant sayings,

to refer to them quickly,

and then in later years,

it is like visiting a forest where you once blazed a trail.

You have the pleasure of going over the old ground,

and recalling both the intellectual scenery

and your own earlier self.

There are of course no friends

like living, breathing, corporeal men and women;

my devotion to reading has never made me a recluse.

How could it?

Books are of the people,

by the people,

for the people.

Literature is the immortal part of history;

it is the best and most enduring part of personality.

But book-friends have this advantage over living friends;

you can enjoy the most truly aristocratic society in the world whenever you want it.

The great dead are beyond our physical reach,

and the great living are usually almost as inaccessible;

as for our personal friends and acquaintances,

we cannot always see them.

Perchance they are asleep, or away on a journey.

But in a private library,

you can at any moment converse with Socrates or Shakespeare

or Carlyle or Dumas or Dickens

or Shaw or Barrie or Galsworthy.

And there is no doubt that in these books

you see these men at their best.

They wrote for *you.*

They "laid themselves out,"

———————————————————

———————————————————

they did their ultimate best to entertain you,

———————————————————

———————————————————

to make a favorable impression.

———————————————————

———————————————————

You are necessary to them as an audience is to an actor;

———————————————————

———————————————————

only instead of seeing them masked,

———————————————————

———————————————————

you look into their innermost heart of heart[s].

Lou Gehrig:

Farewell to Baseball [9, 10]

(272 words)

*T*he New York Yankees honored Lou Gehrig two months after the great first baseman found out that ALS had robbed him of his physical abilities. On July 4, 1939, Yankee Stadium was packed with 61,000 fans.

When the tributes were complete, Gehrig nearly walked away. He had prepared remarks, but wasn't prepared to face his emotions. Shy, he stared at the ground and wiped away tears. Finally, after some encouragement, Gehrig approached the microphones, ran his hand through his hair, took a deep breath, and began to speak without notes:

9. https://www.youtube.com/watch?v=pYyUWn224AE

10. https://www.espn.com/mlb/story/_/id/11159148/mlb-remembering-lou-gehrig-farewell-speech

The Speech

Fans, for the past two weeks you have been reading about the bad break I got. Yet today I consider myself the luckiest man on the face of this earth. I have been in ballparks for seventeen years and have never received anything but kindness and encouragement from you fans.

Look at these grand men. Which of you wouldn't consider it the highlight of his career just to associate with them for even one day? Sure, I'm lucky. Who wouldn't consider it an honor to have known Jacob Ruppert? Also, the builder of baseball's greatest empire, Ed Barrow? To have spent six years with that wonderful little fellow, Miller Huggins? Then to have spent the next nine years with that outstanding leader, that smart student of psychology, the best manager in baseball today, Joe McCarthy? Sure, I'm lucky.

When the New York Giants, a team you would give your right arm to beat, and vice versa, sends you a gift—that's something. When everybody down to the groundskeepers and those boys in white coats remember you with trophies—that's something. When you have a wonderful mother-in-law who takes sides with you in squabbles with her own daughter—that's something. When you have a father and a mother who work all their lives so you can have an education and build your body—it's a blessing. When you have a wife who has been a tower of strength and shown more courage than you dreamed existed—that's the finest I know.

So I close in saying that I may have had a tough break, but I have an awful lot to live for.

Worksheet: Lou Gehrig

_____

_____

Fans,

_____

_____

for the past two weeks you have been reading about the bad break I got.

_____

_____

Yet today I consider myself the luckiest man on the face of this earth.

_____

_____

I have been in ballparks for seventeen years

_____

_____

and have never received anything but kindness and encouragement from you fans.

_____

_____

Look at these grand men.

_____

_____

Which of you wouldn't consider it the highlight of his career just to associate with them for even one day?

_____

_____

Sure, I'm lucky.

_____

_____

Who wouldn't consider it an honor to have known
Jacob Ruppert?

_____

_____

Also, the builder of baseball's greatest empire, Ed Barrow?

_____

_____

To have spent six years with that wonderful little fellow, Miller Huggins?

_____

_____

Then to have spent the next nine years with that outstanding leader,

_____

_____

that smart student of psychology,

_____

_____

the best manager in baseball today,

_____

_____

_____

Joe McCarthy?

_____

Sure, I'm lucky.

_____

_____

When the New York Giants,

_____

_____

a team you would give your right arm to beat,

_____

_____

and vice versa,

_____

_____

sends you a gift—

_____

_____

that's something.

When everybody down to the groundskeepers

and those boys in white coats remember you with trophies—

that's something.

When you have a wonderful mother-in-law who takes sides with you in squabbles with her own daughter—

that's something.

When you have a father and a mother who work all their lives so you can have an education and build your body—

it's a blessing.

—————————————————————————

—————————————————————————

When you have a wife who has been a tower of strength

—————————————————————————

—————————————————————————

and shown more courage than you dreamed existed—

—————————————————————————

—————————————————————————

that's the finest I know.

—————————————————————————

—————————————————————————

So I close in saying

—————————————————————————

—————————————————————————

that I may have had a tough break,

—————————————————————————

—————————————————————————

but I have an awful lot to live for.

General Douglas MacArthur:

Duty, Honor, Country [11, 12]

(385 words)

*M*acArthur's acceptance of the Thayer Award speech before the Corps of Cadets at the U.S. Military Academy at West Point, New York, on May 12, 1962, offers excellent examples of the "rule of threes." Almost every paragraph contains groupings of three elements: "what you ought to be, what you can be, what you will be." There's "music" in this formula; it suggests growing emphasis and rhythmic repetition that builds excitement each time it's used.

11. http://penelope.uchicago.edu/Thayer/E/Gazetteer/Places/America/United_States/Army/USMA/MacArthur/1962_speech_to_the_Corps.html

12. https://www.youtube.com/watch?v=_42_aLGkRpg

The Speech (excerpted)

"Duty, Honor, Country"—those three hallowed words reverently dictate what you ought to be, what you can be, what you will be. They are your rallying point to build courage when courage seems to fail, to regain faith when there seems to be little cause for faith, to create hope when hope becomes forlorn.

Unhappily, I possess neither that eloquence of diction, that poetry of imagination, nor that brilliance of metaphor to tell you all that they mean.

The unbelievers will say they are but words, but a slogan, but a flamboyant phrase. Every pedant, every demagogue, every cynic, every hypocrite, every troublemaker—and, I am sorry to say, some others of an entirely different character—will try to downgrade them even to the extent of mockery and ridicule.

But these are some of the things they do: They build your basic character. They mold you for your future roles as the custodians of the nation's defense. They make you strong enough to know when you are weak, and brave enough to face yourself when you are afraid.

They teach you to be proud and unbending in honest failure, but humble and gentle in success; not to substitute words for action; not to seek the path of comfort, but to face the stress and spur of difficulty and challenge; to learn to stand up in the storm, but to have compassion on those who fall; to master yourself before you seek to master others; to have a heart that is clean, a goal that is high; to learn to laugh, yet never forget how to weep; to reach into the future, yet never neglect the past; to be serious, yet never take yourself too seriously; to be modest so that you will remember the simplicity of true greatness, the open mind of true wisdom, the meekness of true strength.

They give you a temper of the will, a quality of the imagination, a vigor of the emotions, a freshness of the deep springs of life, a temperamental predominance of courage over timidity, an appetite for adventure over love of ease.

They create in your heart the sense of wonder, the unfailing hope of what next, and the joy and inspiration of life. They teach you in this way to be an officer and a gentleman.

Worksheet: Douglas MacArthur

"Duty, Honor, Country"—

those three hallowed words reverently dictate

what you ought to be,

what you can be,

what you will be.

They are your rallying point

to build courage when courage seems to fail,

to regain faith when there seems to be little cause for faith,

to create hope when hope becomes forlorn.

Unhappily, I possess neither that eloquence of diction,

that poetry of imagination,

nor that brilliance of metaphor to tell you all that they mean.

The unbelievers will say they are but words,

but a slogan,

but a flamboyant phrase.

_____

_____

Every pedant,

_____

_____

every demagogue,

_____

_____

every cynic,

_____

_____

every hypocrite,

_____

_____

every troublemaker—

_____

_____

and, I am sorry to say, some others of an entirely different character—

_____

_____

_____

will try to downgrade them even to the extent of mockery and
ridicule.

_____

_____

But these are some of the things they do:

_____

_____

They build your basic character.

_____

_____

They mold you for your future roles as the custodians of the nation's defense.

_____

_____

They make you strong enough to know when you are weak,

_____

_____

and brave enough to face yourself when you are afraid.

_____

_____

They teach you to be proud and unbending in honest failure,

_____

_____

but humble and gentle in success;

_____

_____

not to substitute words for action;

_____

_____

not to seek the path of comfort,

_____

_____

but to face the stress and spur of difficulty and challenge;

_____

_____

to learn to stand up in the storm,

_____

_____

_____

but to have compassion on those who fall;

_____

_____

to master yourself before you seek to master others;

_____

_____

to have a heart that is clean,

_____

_____

a goal that is high;

_____

_____

to learn to laugh,

yet never forget how to weep;

to reach into the future, yet never neglect the past;

to be serious, yet never take yourself too seriously;

to be modest

so that you will remember the simplicity of true greatness,

the open mind of true wisdom,

the meekness of true strength.

They give you a temper of the will,

_____

_____

a quality of the imagination,

_____

_____

a vigor of the emotions,

_____

_____

a freshness of the deep springs of life,

_____

_____

a temperamental predominance of courage over timidity,

_____

_____

an appetite for adventure over love of ease.

_____

_____

They create in your heart the sense of wonder,

_____

_____

the unfailing hope of what next,

_____

_____

and the joy and inspiration of life.

_____

_____

They teach you in this way

_____

_____

to be an officer and a gentleman.

Patrick Henry:
Give Me Liberty or Give Me Death [13]

(366 words)

*P*atrick Henry gave his famous speech to the Second Virginia Convention on March 23, 1775, at St. John's Church in Richmond, Virginia, which convinced the convention to muster troops for the Revolutionary War.

According to Edmund Randolph, the convention sat in silence for several minutes afterward. Thomas Marshall stated that the speech was "one of the boldest, vehement, and animated pieces of eloquence that had ever been delivered." George Mason said, "Every word he says not only engages but commands the attention, and your passions are no longer your own when he addresses them."

13. https://www.history.org/almanack/life/politics/giveme.cfm

Eyewitness Account

Senator John Roane witnessed the speech. His description[14] is worthy of recounting:

"You remember, sir, the conclusion of the speech, so often declaimed in various ways by school-boys — 'Is life so dear, or peace so sweet, as to be purchased at the price of chains and slavery? Forbid it, Almighty God! I know not what course others may take, but as for me, give me liberty, or give me death!' He gave each of these words a meaning which is not conveyed by the reading or delivery of them in the ordinary way. When he said, 'Is life so dear, or peace so sweet, as to be purchased at the price of chains and slavery?' he stood in the attitude of a condemned galley slave, loaded with fetters, awaiting his doom. His form was bowed; his wrists were crossed; his manacles were almost visible as he stood like an embodiment of helplessness and agony. After a solemn pause, he raised his eyes and chained hands towards heaven, and prayed, in words and tones which thrilled every heart, 'Forbid it, Almighty God!' He then turned towards the timid loyalists of the House, who were quaking with terror at the idea of the consequences of participating in proceedings which would be visited with the penalties of treason by the British crown; and he

14. https://www.varsitytutors.com/ebooks/earlyamerica/PatrickHenry/tyl-erm2936829368-8.pdf

slowly bent his form yet nearer to the earth, and said, 'I know not what course others may take,' and he accompanied the words with his hands still crossed, while he seemed to be weighed down with additional chains. The man appeared transformed into an oppressed, heart-broken, and hopeless felon. After remaining in this posture of humiliation long enough to impress the imagination with the condition of the colony under the iron heel of military despotism, he arose proudly, and exclaimed, 'but as for me,'—and the words hissed through his clenched teeth, while his body was thrown back, and every muscle and tendon was strained against the fetters which bound him, and, with his countenance distorted by agony and rage, he looked for a moment like Laocoön in a death struggle with coiling serpents; then the loud, clear, triumphant notes, 'Give me liberty,' electrified the assembly. It was not a prayer, but a stern demand, which would submit to no refusal or delay. The sound of his voice, as he spoke these memorable words, was like that of a Spartan pæan on the field of Platæa; and, as each syllable of the word 'liberty' echoed through the building, his fetters were shivered; his arms were hurled apart; and the links of his chains were scattered to the winds. When he spoke the word 'liberty' with an emphasis never given it before, his hands were open, and his arms elevated and extended; his countenance was radiant; he stood erect and defiant; while the sound of his voice and the sublimity of his attitude made him appear a magnificent incarnation of Freedom, and expressed all that can be acquired or enjoyed by nations and individuals invincible and free. After a momentary pause, only long enough to permit the echo of the word 'liberty' to cease, he let his left hand fall powerless to his side, and clenched his right hand firmly, as if holding a dagger with the point aimed at his breast. He stood like a Roman senator defying Cæsar, while the unconquerable spirit of Cato of Utica flashed from every feature; and he closed the grand appeal with the solemn words, 'or give me death!' which sounded with the awful cadence of a hero's dirge, fearless of death, and victorious in death; and he suited the action to the word by a blow upon the left breast with the right hand, which seemed to drive the dagger to the patriot's heart."

The Speech (excerpted)

They tell us, sir, that we are weak; unable to cope with so formidable an adversary. But when shall we be stronger? Will it be the next week, or the next year? Will it be when we are totally disarmed, and when a British guard shall be stationed in every house? Shall we gather strength by irresolution and inaction? Shall we acquire the means of effectual resistance, by lying supinely on our backs, and hugging the delusive phantom of hope, until our enemies shall have bound us hand and foot? Sir, we are not weak if we make a proper use of those means which the God of nature hath placed in our power. Three millions of people, armed in the holy cause of liberty, and in such a country as that which we possess, are invincible by any force which our enemy can send against us. Besides, sir, we shall not fight our battles alone. There is a just God who presides over the destinies of nations; and who will raise up friends to fight our battles for us. The battle, sir, is not to the strong alone; it is to the vigilant, the active, the brave. Besides, sir, we have no election. If we were base enough to desire it, it is now too late to retire from the contest. There is no retreat but in submission and slavery! Our chains are forged! Their clanking may be heard on the plains of Boston! The war is inevitable and let it come! I repeat it, sir, let it come.

It is in vain, sir, to extenuate the matter. Gentlemen may cry, Peace, Peace but there is no peace. The war is actually begun! The next gale that sweeps from the north will bring to our ears the clash of resounding arms! Our brethren are already in the field! Why stand we here idle? What is it that gentlemen wish? What would they have? Is life so dear, or peace so sweet, as to be purchased at the price of chains and slavery? Forbid it, Almighty God! I know not what course others may take; but as for me, give me liberty or give me death!

Worksheet: Patrick Henry

_____

_____

They tell us, sir, that we are weak;

_____

_____

unable to cope with so formidable an adversary.

_____

_____

But when shall we be stronger?

_____

_____

Will it be the next week, or the next year?

_____

_____

Will it be when we are totally disarmed,

_____

_____

and when a British guard shall be stationed in every house?

_____

_____

Shall we gather strength by irresolution and inaction?

_____

_____

Shall we acquire the means of effectual resistance,

_____

_____

by lying supinely on our backs,

_____

_____

and hugging the delusive phantom of hope,

_____

_____

until our enemies shall have bound us hand and foot?

_____

_____

Sir, we are not weak if we make a proper use of those means which the God of nature hath placed in our power.

_____

_____

Three millions of people,

_____

_____

armed in the holy cause of liberty,

_____

_____

and in such a country as that which we possess,

_____

_____

are invincible by any force which our enemy can send against us.

_____

_____

Besides, sir, we shall not fight our battles alone.

_____

_____

There is a just God who presides over the destinies of nations;

_____

_____

and who will raise up friends to fight our battles for us.

_____

_____

The battle, sir, is not to the strong alone;

_____

_____

it is to the vigilant,

_____

_____

the active,

_____

_____

the brave.

_____

_____

Besides, sir, we have no election.

_____

_____

If we were base enough to desire it,

_____

_____

it is now too late to retire from the contest.

_____

_____

There is no retreat but in submission and slavery!

_____

_____

_____

Our chains are forged!

_____

_____

Their clanking may be heard on the plains of Boston!

_____

_____

The war is inevitable and let it come!

_____

_____

I repeat it, sir, let it come.

It is in vain, sir, to extenuate the matter.

Gentlemen may cry, Peace, Peace but there is no peace.

The war is actually begun!

The next gale that sweeps from the north will bring to our ears the clash of resounding arms!

Our brethren are already in the field!

Why stand we here idle?

What is it that gentlemen wish?

What would they have?

_____

_____

Is life so dear, or peace so sweet,

_____

_____

as to be purchased at the price of chains and slavery?

_____

_____

Forbid it, Almighty God!

_____

_____

I know not what course others may take;

_____

_____

but as for me, give me liberty or give me death!

Susan B Anthony:

Are Women Persons?[15]

(238 words)

S usan B. Anthony had been arrested for voting in Rochester, New York in the 1872 elections, violating state laws that allowed only men to vote. During her criminal trial, Anthony argued that she had the right to vote because the recently adopted Fourteenth Amendment to the U.S. Constitution read, "No State shall make or enforce any law which shall abridge the privileges or immunities of citizens of the United States." On the final day of the trial, Judge Hunt asked Anthony if she had anything to say. She responded with the most famous speech in the history of the agitation for women's suffrage.

15. http://www.historyplace.com/speeches/anthony.htm

The Speech (excerpted)

Friends and fellow citizens: I stand before you tonight under indictment for the alleged crime of having voted at the last presidential election, without having a lawful right to vote. It shall be my work this evening to prove to you that in thus voting, I not only committed no crime, but, instead, simply exercised my citizen's rights, guaranteed to me and all United States citizens by the National Constitution, beyond the power of any state to deny.

The preamble of the Federal Constitution says:

"We, the people of the United States, in order to form a more perfect union, establish justice, insure domestic tranquility, provide for the common defense, promote the general welfare, and secure the blessings of liberty to ourselves and our posterity, do ordain and establish this Constitution for the United States of America."

It was we, the people; not we, the white male citizens; nor yet we, the male citizens; but we, the whole people, who formed the Union. And we formed it, not to give the blessings of liberty, but to secure them; not to the half of ourselves and the half of our posterity, but to the whole people—women as well as men. And it is a downright mockery to talk to women of their enjoyment of the blessings of liberty while they are denied the use of the only means of securing them provided by this Democratic-Republican government—the ballot.

Worksheet: Susan B. Anthony

_____

_____

Friends and fellow citizens:

_____

_____

I stand before you tonight under indictment for the alleged crime of having voted at the last presidential election,

_____

_____

without having a lawful right to vote.

_____

_____

It shall be my work this evening to prove to you that in thus voting,

_____

_____

I not only committed no crime,

_____

_____

but, instead, simply exercised my citizen's rights,

_____

_____

guaranteed to me and all United States citizens

_____

_____

by the National Constitution,

_____

_____

beyond the power of any state to deny.

_____

The preamble of the Federal Constitution says:

_____

_____

"We, the people of the United States,

_____

_____

in order to form a more perfect union,

_____

_____

establish justice,

_____

_____

insure domestic tranquility,

_____

_____

provide for the common defense,

_____

_____

promote the general welfare,

_____

_____

and secure the blessings of liberty to ourselves and our posterity,

_____

_____

do ordain and establish this Constitution

_____

_____

for the United States of America."

_____

_____

It was we, the people;

_____

not we, the white male citizens;

_____

nor yet we, the male citizens;

_____

but we, the whole people,

_____

_____

who formed the Union.

_____

_____

And we formed it, not to give the blessings of liberty, but to secure them;

_____

_____

not to the half of ourselves and the half of our posterity, but to the whole people—

_____

_____

women as well as men.

_____

_____

And it is a downright mockery to talk to women of their enjoyment of the blessings of liberty

_____

_____

while they are denied the use of the only means of securing them provided by this Democratic-Republican government—

_____

_____

the ballot.

Sojourner Truth:
Ain't I a Woman?[16]

(353 words)

"Ain't I a Woman?" was an extemporaneous speech given by Sojourner Truth (1797–1883), who was born into slavery in New York State. After gaining her freedom in 1827, she became a well-known anti-slavery speaker. This address was given at a women's convention in Akron, Ohio on May 29, 1851.

The Speech

Well, children, where there is so much racket there must be something out of kilter. I think that 'twixt the negroes of the South and the women at the North, all talking about rights, the white men will be in a fix pretty soon. But what's all this here talking about?

16. https://www.nps.gov/articles/sojourner-truth.htm

That man over there says that women need to be helped into carriages, and lifted over ditches, and to have the best place everywhere. Nobody ever helps me into carriages, or over mud-puddles, or gives me any best place! And ain't I a woman? Look at me! Look at my arm! I have ploughed and planted, and gathered into barns, and no man could head me! And ain't I a woman? I could work as much and eat as much as a man—when I could get it—and bear the lash as well! And ain't I a woman? I have borne thirteen children, and seen most all sold off to slavery, and when I cried out with my mother's grief, none but Jesus heard me! And ain't I a woman?

Then they talk about this thing in the head; what's this they call it? [member of audience whispers, "intellect"] That's it, honey. What's that got to do with women's rights or negroes' rights? If my cup won't hold but a pint, and yours holds a quart, wouldn't you be mean not to let me have my little half-measure full?

Then that little man in black there, he says women can't have as much rights as men, 'cause Christ wasn't a woman! Where did your Christ come from? Where did your Christ come from? From God and a woman! Man had nothing to do with Him.

If the first woman God ever made was strong enough to turn the world upside down all alone, these women together ought to be able to turn it back, and get it right side up again! And now they is asking to do it; the men better let them.

Obliged to you for hearing me, and now old Sojourner ain't got nothing more to say.

Worksheet: Sojourner Truth

_____

_____

Well, children,

_____

_____

where there is so much racket there must be something out of kilter.

_____

_____

I think that 'twixt the negroes of the South and the women at the North, all talking about rights,

_____

_____

the white men will be in a fix pretty soon.

_____

_____

But what's all this here talking about?

_____

_____

That man over there says that women need to be helped into carriages, and lifted over ditches,

and to have the best place everywhere.

Nobody ever helps me into carriages,

or over mud-puddles,

or gives me any best place!

And ain't I a woman?

Look at me!

Look at my arm!

I have ploughed and planted,

and gathered into barns,

and no man could head me!

And ain't I a woman?

I could work as much and eat as much as a man—

when I could get it—

and bear the lash as well!

And ain't I a woman?

I have borne thirteen children,

and seen most all sold off to slavery,

and when I cried out with my mother's grief,

none but Jesus heard me!

And ain't I a woman?

Then they talk about this thing in the head;

what's this they call it?

Intellect? That's it, honey.

What's that got to do with women's rights or negroes' rights?

If my cup won't hold but a pint, and yours holds a quart,

wouldn't you be mean not to let me have my little half-measure full?

Then that little man in black there,

he says women can't have as much rights as men,

'cause Christ wasn't a woman!

Where did your Christ come from?

Where did your Christ come from?

_____

_____

From God and a woman!

_____

_____

Man had nothing to do with Him.

_____

_____

   If the first woman God ever made

_____

_____

was strong enough to turn the world upside down all alone,

_____

_____

these women together ought to be able to turn it back,

_____

_____

and get it right side up again!

_____

_____

And now they is asking to do it;

_____

_____

the men better let them.

_____

_____

Obliged to you for hearing me,

_____

_____

and now old Sojourner ain't got nothing more to say.

Final Exercise

*H*aving worked through ten speeches and ten speakers, you've thought about pauses, emphasis words, and gestures. You've called on the people to defend their homeland, pleaded for dignity, and honored the fallen. You've explored the heights of eloquence and demanded fairness and respect in common language.

It's your turn to inspire people—one or millions—to think, feel, and act to make the world a better place. Such is the power of the capable orator. Use yours well.

— Dave Bricker, November, 2019

About the Author

Dave Bricker is a speaker, author, and designer based in Miami, Florida. Through his company, Remarkable Stories, Inc. he teaches the art of business transformation through storytelling to writers, speakers, professionals, and visionaries.

Learn about Dave Bricker's speaking, training, and coaching programs, and subscribe to the StorySailing® newsletter at https://storysailing.com.

Other Books by Dave Bricker

The Dance: A Novel

Waves: A Novel

Currents: A Novel

The One-Hour Guide to Self-Publishing

The Writer's Guide to Powerful Prose

The Blue Monk

The Publisher's Guide to Book Anatomy

The Story Story: A Voyage Through the Islands of Connection
  & Engagement

StorySailing: A Guide to Storytelling for Speakers, Trainers,
  and Coaches

Death of the Guitar: Collected Stories, Poems, and Sketches

Because independent writers and publishers should be held to the same high standards as the mainstream publishing industry, I encourage you to post an honest and objective review of this book on Amazon.com or the online bookstore of your choice.

Thank you,

—Dave Bricker

www.ingramcontent.com/pod-product-compliance
Lightning Source LLC
Chambersburg PA
CBHW050800250626
47155CB00005B/2148